# Praises for Don't Forget Your Pearls

Rickesha shares her story as a strong woman, who has been through a lot but found a way to find blessings in the lessons of life. Her story is raw and a true testimony that can motivate others to be positive about their trials and tribulations. Rickesha can offer a lot to the world through her story, including how to live in your truth and be unapologetic about your journey. Your journey can make or break you, and Rickesha shows how to use your journey to shape you into the person you were meant to be.

-T. Lundy

RICKESHA ROSE

# Don't Forget Your Pearls

"*A Tribute to a Woman's Worth*"

RICKESHA ROSE

RICKESHA ROSE

## *Dedication*

To my children, Terry & Ter'Mya it is not until you become a parent, that you truly understand the love I have that breathes for you, no sacrifice too big or small to see you smile. As you guys grow my sole goal as your mother is to show you more, that your more than any statistic that was ever put on your name. I refuse to settle in life so that settling will not be apart of the greatness that exists in you. My prayer is that you take the sharing of my story and my experiences, as wisdom, that no confusion and no cycles be repeated. Your lives have a purpose!

To my mother and sister, I pray that the sharing of my testimony becomes the encouragement to unlock the stories inside of you.

RICKESHA ROSE

# Epigraph

"It is imperative that you take what is necessary for your journey ahead."

RICKESHA ROSE

# Foreword

Growing up I was always into fairy tales and love stories. I learned from watching movies that, pearls have always represented a sense of elegance, importance, and royalty. This resonated with me, growing up. The color white has always represented purity and beauty. In every fairy tale, the mother of the bride would place pearls around her daughter's neck, before she walked down the aisle. The pearls were always the final accessory that was passed down from generation to generation. With the passing of the pearls came a speech.

Today marks the first day of the rest of your life. Today, I give you pearls of wisdom. I give you elegance to illuminate the beauty that already exists. In these pearls, there is strength, value, and honor as you prepare to move into a new season in your life.

In a perfect fairy tale, the bride would, take the pearls and live her happily ever after, for she has everything she needs, wrapped in her string of pearls. I share this with you as I want you to be actively thinking about what lessons are most important on your string of pearls? What are the treasures that help you get to your happily ever after?

Pearls represent elegance and grace in a woman's life. Pearls, represent beauty, value, and the final touch that brings everything in one's attire together, before heading out to the "ball." Pearls have been a representation of value since the beginning of time.

**Matthew 7:6**

"Do not give dogs what is sacred; do not throw your pearls before swine.

Pearls are known as the "Queen of Gems." Unlike gemstones that are mined from the earth, a living organism produces a pearl, making their existence rare in nature. Similar to the pearl, what you build around you, becomes the essence of who you are. Your values and your true beliefs are your outer shell. Many times our outer shells, or walls develop from a place of hurt, disappointment, or heartbreak. These factors force us to hide who we are, and the innocence that was once within us.

# Preface

I was in a middle school health class teaching a curriculum on how to adjust to being a middle school student. The curriculum dealt with self-esteem, peer pressure, and conflict resolution. By that time, I had been teaching and speaking to youth for many years. The words to whatever we were covering naturally flowed, and on occasion, I use personal examples. The students found humor in my examples. Although in many ways, they could relate, they struggled with believing that I had struggled with anything. I stood before them, well educated, well dressed, and full of confidence. Even so, I had struggled.

I spoke these words...

"Whenever you use something in a different manner than what its purpose is, the effects are dangerous." We were discussing the use of chemicals being used outside of their purpose. For example, cleaning products being used for huffing. As I stood in front of that class my words resonated within me, and I found myself replaying their meaning in my head. I began to reflect on my life. I had a purpose, and I knew that operating outside of my purpose, affected me in a dangerous way. It was an uncomfortable place. There had been a time in my life where "operating in purpose" was a foreign concept to me. Growing up, I had never heard of people having a purpose. Living a life with no understanding of purpose, often left me spinning my wheels. I did not understand why I felt so uncomfortable when trying to fit in. In this space, things never turned out exactly how I wanted them to.

Now, speaking to the class, I recognized that I knew the difference. I felt the difference. Anytime I was chasing something that gave me purpose it came with peace. I had managed to discover this peace when I first started mentoring and speaking. I often questioned if I was qualified to serve in such a capacity, as my behind the scenes life inclusive of my finances, and relationships needed help. The feedback I'd received always told a different story. Testimonials about how connections with me changed lives were reinforcement. People were growing right before my eyes, many times from my words alone. Some of those words, I didn't even remember speaking into their lives. I knew that I had a purpose to fulfill. I knew It was bigger than me, the first time a student told me, that I was the only reason that they didn't give up.

This, was not always the case. The first time I shared my story, I had no idea that it would be heard by so many people. The first time, I was completely vulnerable in a small Bible study group, designed specifically to help women who were survivors of domestic violence. The women were so receptive and connected to my story. In it, they heard the pain, but more importantly, they saw the victory. There were times that I would be speaking words with no idea how many people were listening, watching and connecting. I share with my audiences today from a different perspective. As I look back and reflect on the lessons that I've learned throughout my journey, I realize that our words do have power.

RICKESHA ROSE

# Acknowledgements

Tremendous thanks, Ardre Orie, and the 13th and Joan Publishing Team, thank you for accepting the challenge, and helping me release the story inside of me.

To all of my family for your unwavering love and support. There are far too many of you for me to name individually, but to my siblings Tevorace, Temisha, Ricky, Rickeam, and Ricktavious, and brother in law John, as long as there's breath in my body you will always have a sister in me to push you to concur your biggest fears. To my Aunts, Uncles, my nieces & nephews, and all of my wonderful cousins, I love you more than you could ever fully process. Your support was never in vain.

Thank you to my very best friend, Parmaisha aka my 'Top Notch', your unquestioned loyalty and friendship has held me through the decades.

To Tray, your benevolence and ardent support of all things is greatly appreciated.

To every student and young girl who has ever crossed my threshold and consulted in me. my success is directly tied to all of you. Thank you so very much.

To my *mother,* Ursula, your tough love, your sacrifices, your strong will has taught me so much, your sacrifices have not gone unnoticed

To my father in heaven, Ricky Sr. I miss you more than anyone could have ever imagine, the positive energy you left behind, ignited my soul to travel and discover what the world hold for me.

To anyone who has ever encouraged me in any way, your words did not fall on dry soil. Because of you I believed in me, so for that I thank you.

## Introduction

It is not always what we forget, but why we have forgotten that must be considered. There are situations in our lives that force us to attempt to recall and to remember lessons of the past.

After having my son, much of my life became a blur. My ability to recollect has only gotten worse over time. I've forgotten items, places, people and even moments in time. I've been continuously scorned by family members, and friends for forgetting simple things like them telling me to lock the door, or to bring items, or to take items to an intended destination. No matter how much I tried, I always seemed to forget.

As I matured as a woman, forgetting became a strategy for sustaining my happiness, sense of peace, dignity, and my values. Forgetting became a part of who I was. If someone were to ask me who I was in the year 2015, I would not be able to tell them. My mind was in a battle with who I was becoming, and the things that I had forgotten.

If I were to be asked where my pearls were during that era of my life, I wouldn't be able to tell them. There were so many lessons that mattered in the situations that I needed to come out of that I had forgotten. I had forgotten so much that I was on the verge of losing myself.

RICKESHA ROSE

## Author's Prayer

Dear Heavenly Father,

I pray that the words on these pages serve as knowledge, peace, hope, and represent your light. I thank you for everything that you've done, everything you're doing and everything you are going to do in my life, and in the lives of those who allow these words to resonate in their hearts. Amen.

RICKESHA ROSE

## Table of Contents

Foreword ............................................................. 9
Preface ................................................................ 11
Acknowledgements ........................................... 15
Introduction ....................................................... 17
Author's Prayer ................................................. 19
Prologue ............................................................. 23
An Open Letter To My Younger Self ............... 29
Disclosure .......................................................... 31

| | | |
|---|---|---|
| Chapter 1 | Baby, I got You ................................ | 33 |
| Chapter 2 | High School Is Over ....................... | 39 |
| Chapter 3 | Jail Time .......................................... | 42 |
| Chapter 4 | Rollercoaster And Red Flags ......... | 47 |
| Chapter 5 | Recovery And Ring ........................ | 51 |
| Chapter 6 | Happy Ever…Maybe ....................... | 54 |
| Chapter 7 | Numb ................................................ | 58 |
| Chapter 8 | I Had To Run .................................. | 62 |

| | | |
|---|---|---|
| Chapter 9 | Last Straw | 65 |
| Chapter 10 | Go Your Way | 67 |
| Chapter 11 | Final Straw | 69 |
| Chapter 12 | Surrender | 72 |
| Conclusion | | 77 |
| About The Author | | 85 |
| Connect With Rickesha Rose | | 86 |

# Prologue

It was graduation day, and for the average seventeen-year-old, this was supposed to be the happiest time of my life. It was May 2007 at St.Lucie Fairground. I was hot and bothered by the wait like most of the graduates, of Fort Pierce Central High. I just knew that I was going to pass out before I made it to shake the principal and assistant principal's hands, as they congratulated each of us on reaching this significant milestone in life. I was indeed happy to have been graduating, as it had been in question as to if I would even make it.

In September 2005, the beginning of my junior year, I had given birth to my firstborn. After the birth of my son, I was on hospital homebound for the first quarter of my junior year. When I returned to school, there were some differences of opinion from some of my teachers about what I should be given credit for. My mom called a meeting with the Assistant Principal after I had been told by a few teachers that I was going to fail. I had completed work while I was homeschooled, but for whatever reason what I did outside of school, did not transfer back to the courses I had begun taking, before being out. It was as if I had started the class, left for two months and then returned. Lucky for me, my track record as a student had never been in question before. I had always been an honor roll student. My mom and Mr.

Beauchamp (the assistant principal) fought on my behalf. They were able to convince the toughest teachers, to take into consideration the work I did before leaving, and the work I was willing to put in to receive a satisfactory grade. I received an incomplete status until I proved myself worthy, of getting the A's and B's I had always earned. This was just the beginning.

Having a child and returning back to my regular school, also meant that I couldn't expect things to come easy for me, or for teachers to care.

At graduation, my mother, father, siblings, aunts, and closest cousins sat in the audience, patiently waiting for me to walk across the stage. I can't say that I hadn't been a disappointment to them but I believed that I was also a disappointment to the father of my son's family as well. I'm sure that on that day, they were happy for me. Everyone had been very supportive, helping me get through school, stepping in and helping out on the days when school and being a mother was too much to handle. Many days I would wake up from a nap to find my son with my mom. Sitting with my mother in the audience was my was my whole life, packaged as the being that grew inside of me when I was just fifteen years old. My son, then just year and a half, was born Sept 5. He knew no pain and no judgment. He was unaware that his mother was just a teen. He never had the opportunity to question if his teen mother would be able to sufficiently provide for him. He was completely innocent and worth every fight to give him the best life possible. He was the center of my world.

Even though I had become a mother, I had also managed to push through the second half of my junior year and complete my senior year. That was the reason that I stood in preparation to receive my diploma. I learned that if I work hard, I could accomplish so much. Obstacles only pushed me to go harder. I had more at stake than my peers.

As I stood there, I felt the onset of nausea. Mrs. Beauchamp, the assistant principal stood at the stairway between the line of graduates and the stage. "Are You ok," she asked? Her sweet voice prompted a smile from me. I held on tightly as she grabbed my hand, and I leaned in toward her. I needed that moment to rest. I just knew that the very thing that haunted me since I was a little girl was going to happen. I knew that I was going to faint in front of everyone. I had fainted once when I was a cheerleader for Pop Warner, a youth athletic league. Even though I distinctly remember the event, my family never let me outlive it. They would joke with me and say, "you know you need to sit down, you know you liable to faint." They would often refer to this statement about me doing anything physical or being outside. Later in life, I discovered just how much I had accomplished and risked to prove others wrong.

My senior year of high school I made the decision to run track, I was not a fast runner, but I knew how to get over hurdles. I learned how to position myself so that even if I didn't win the race, I didn't fall. Falling was always the hardest part. If I fell, I always got up. The problem with falling is that you immediately feel like you've lost. You then spend the rest of your time attempting to recover from the fall. When I ran, track it shocked my entire family. They told me my whole life that I'd never play sports because I couldn't be in the sun too long. It wasn't until high school that I discovered that my mother shielded me from excessive physical activity, due to me having a heart murmur. I was well in my 20's the first time I learned that I spent quite a bit of time in the hospital as a baby because of my heart condition. As I look back over my life, jumping hurdles prepared me for more than I could ever imagine.

Luckily, on graduation day, I found the strength to walk across that stage, with my head held high. On the other side of that stage, was life after high school.

Little did I know, that sweltering day in May, just how dangerous crossing that stage would be. It represented another transition in my life. Everything that our teachers and loved ones had imparted in us was meant to prepare us for what awaited on the other side of high school. Most of us were preparing for college, the military, parties, and to get out of our parents' homes. Whatever independence and freedom we could find, we were all seeking it. I was preparing to take care of my son, and unbeknownst to me to give birth to his baby sister.

I was graduating high school at the age of seventeen, with a baby in the audience, and one on the way. This was my life now. I struggled to prepare for what others said my life would be like. I struggled to prepare for the things they said I no longer had the option to do. I mean I heard them, I was wise enough to know that my life would be different and that I needed to prepare for a path much different from my fellow classmates.

After graduation, the day to day hustle began. I secured a job and started classes at Indian River Community College. Determined to not to allow my circumstances to make me feel any less than my peers, I put my education first and my job second. I began to navigate the working field and college life. I would work during the day, get off spending a few hours with the kids, which included getting them ready for grandma's house, then I would head to my night classes. I went head first, non-stop, starting with just a few classes and working my way up to attending full-time, changing jobs when necessary. I worked jobs at night, overnight, in between classes and whatever else was needed. I only worked in positions that allowed me to go to school. I was working hard, and I was struggling, but I was committed to that college graduate dream if that was what it took to give my children the world. I was all in.

RICKESHA ROSE

# An Open Letter to My Younger Self

Dear Younger Me,

You are going to be ok. You will have some tough days ahead of you. You will encounter some hard times. You won't always make the right decisions. You will find your way. Be sure to take your time. Be slow to speak and mindful to listen. I want you to know that God has your best intentions in mind, and you have nothing to prove. You're going to hear some things that are going to hurt. You will make some mistakes, and do some things out of anger. Never forget that God will take care of you. You will birth greatness, and you too will be great. Take your time to discover yourself, and remember that anything worth having is worth waiting for. You are the daughter of a King. No man or woman can change who you are to God. The late nights and early mornings that you endure will shape you. The heartbreak and tears will teach and mold you. Every battle is not yours to fight. You are strong enough to withstand it all but graced for so much more. Hold your crown tightly and stay focused. Everything that you need to be the woman you were proposed to be is already inside of you.

Signed,
Another Year Wiser
Rickesha

RICKESHA ROSE

# Disclosure

Names have been changed to protect their identity. It is not my attention to point fingers or to make anyone out to be the bad guy. I share these intimate parts of my life to encourage and inspire anyone who is experiencing these cycles or who have walked down a similar path. This is my #Metoo. I celebrate the woman I am now, knowing all of the things I've overcome. Lessons learned have become lessons to be shared. I pray that my story is seen as a testimony to demonstrate that your past does not dictate your present. I have invited you along on this journey with me. I ask that you have an open mind and that you guard your heart, this is my journey to Becoming Concrete.

RICKESHA ROSE

## Chapter One

*"Sometimes we just need to hear that everything is ok, even if it's not."*

-Rickesha Rose-

"What the hell are you going to do with another baby," my mother asked as she stood in front of her bathroom. Already months along I stood still, as the tears began to fall, I murmured, "I'm going to take care of it." The room fell silent, as my mother put her head down. I knew I was dismissed. I don't know why I would have been expecting any other reaction. After all, her baby girl was now pregnant with a second child. My thoughts ran wild ...what was I going to do with another baby? I knew that I could not stay there. I would have to leave. I made the decision to move out. My 17-year-old mind ran wild. I felt moving out would make the perception of me being an adult better. I thought that doing so would give me responsibility. Besides my bedroom inside my mother's home did not seem appropriate for myself and two kids. I was quick on my feet when it came to solving problems. After all, this wasn't my first hurdle. I couldn't afford to think negatively. This baby was on the way. I contemplated that Deon was working now, and so was I. I needed to call him. "Hello," Hey Deon," "what's up baby? "Nothing! What you doing," I said in a low tone to let him know something was wrong. "Nothing, just sitting at the house. What's up with you? Coming over here?" "Yeah."

"Come on Dj, we're going to see daddy." Deon Jr., our two-year-old was sitting on the bunk bed, playing with his toy car. Dj jumped up with excitement and ran to get his shoes, from by the door. I quickly noticed as he stood puzzled, holding only one shoe with no matching shoe in sight. "Come on Dj, it's in the car," I remembered bringing him in with only one shoe on. Since I had become a mother, I was always forgetting or losing something, especially in transition from one place to another.

When I arrived at Deon's house, he met me outside. Still upset & teary-eyed, I sat in the car, as if I wasn't getting out. He came to the driver's side and leaned over into the car. "What's wrong with you?" "I will tell you later," motioning my head toward the back seat. Deon went to open the back door "Hey daddy's man!" Dj began to laugh, and they immediately initiated their routine of play fighting and making each other laugh. "Hey, let's go see your uncle." Deon proceeds to take Dj into the house. Usually, I follow behind but today we needed to talk, and he needed to know it was severe. Me staying back was code to let Dj play. I was sure his nana was also in the house. She and Dj were pretty close, so she loved when he came over.

When Deon returned, I was leaning against the car. Everything about my posture said we had a problem. "What's wrong," he said in his daddy's voice as if I was a baby. He put his arms around me, and we just hugged for a second. "I can't stay there anymore," I whispered softly. "Why? What happened?" "I told her!" "Told her what?" "I'm pregnant Deon!" "You took the test?" "I don't need proof, Deon."

We had already had a conversation about the possibility, but we had really been ignoring the reality. I was well over four months, but I was small. He began to rub my stomach. "What you want to do?" "Move! This all your fault!" Smiling, he pulled me closer and grabbed me and held me close. I rested my head on his chest. He said the very words I needed to hear "I got you. I got us." Those words gave me hope. At that moment, it was everything I needed to hear.

Deon and I had started dating when I was just fourteen. He was sixteen. We were the definition of puppy love. One thing that I really loved about him was that he never pressured me into anything. When we first started dating, I had not been sexually active, and even though he had, he never compelled me. It was my own curiosity at the age of fifteen that led to the pregnancy of our first-born, Deon Jr. Now we were like any other teen couple. The love for the child that we created trumped every encounter we were facing as young parents. Deon and I had met when we were in middle school. We rode the same bus, and he and his friends were always in the back of the bus, making jokes and making everyone laugh. I was pretty quiet in middle school and kept to myself, so I had to really like something about you for me to open up. It wasn't until my eighth grade year that Deon and I connected for the first time. I had spilled my guts to my best friend that I liked him. For whatever reason, she took that as an open invitation to hook us up. He reached out to me and told me straight up "your homegirl told me what you said." I was ashamed, embarrassed, and excited at the same time. It was something I couldn't have told him myself. I had one of those "girl I can't believe you, but thanks" moments with my best friend. Due to him being in high school and me being in middle school, that flame didn't last long. My older brother and his best friends who attended school with Deon, did what big brothers do. They told me that I didn't know what he was doing, as we were at different schools, and that no boy in high school had good intentions with a girl in middle school. My brother's friends who were just extended brothers to me gave me the talk about expectations from high school guys. I decided to let it go, they were right. Besides, we only talked on the phone, so it was limited, and my mother had not given me the ok to have a boyfriend.

The next year, Deon and I reconnected when I got into high school. With the little sense, I thought I had about guys, he seemed like the safest choice. From the ninth to tenth grade, we did what high school sweethearts do. It wasn't long before we were telling each other that we loved each other. We were getting closer and closer emotionally and physically. My parents hated it, and my mother had been very open about him no longer seeing me. She banned him from coming to our home. That ban just made me rebellious, and what started out as something innocent began to escalate. Sneaking around to see each other only opened the doors for sex. Teenage hormones told my mind that since we were already alone, we had nothing but time and opportunity on our hands.

The first time my mother discovered I was having sex, she said to me "don't get pregnant." That was literally it. It wasn't in the kindest tone or in a mood that suggested it was ok. Three months after those exact words, I was expecting my firstborn child from the first guy I had ever had sex with.

We definitely had our work cut out for us. This was before shows like Teen Mom, 16 and Pregnant existed. People connected with the people on those shows. The world was able to learn their stories, feel a sense of empathy and share compassion for the young mothers. Me on the other hand, I got the stares in the store, heard the whispers all around, and I encountered the judgments first hand. I had gotten used to being looked at differently. Something stood out about me my whole life. I was born with a birthmark on my face, which never bothered me until I was in grade school. I honestly never knew I was different until people began to ask questions like

"What happened to your face?" They would say things like, "You look like you got beat up." My natural beauty mark laid right underneath my eye. It wasn't long before the name "black eye" became the laughing joke among my peers. I could distinctly remember kids trying to touch my face as if they couldn't believe what they were looking at. I was almost an adult before I realized that I was bullied as a child. For whatever reason, I had tough skin. It never bothered me unless someone close to me mentioned it. Nevertheless, I was up for the challenge. Now, with child, being stared at or looked at differently was old news to me. I wasn't the first teen mom, and I wouldn't be the last. I knew I had a lot to learn. Learning was one of my strengths.

# Chapter Two

*"You never know what the future holds, unless you decide to create it yourself."*
-Rickesha Rose

It was the summer of 2007, and I had just graduated from high school. As I sat and looked through my scrapbook, I was pretty proud of the things I had done in during my senior year. Except for having a toddler, I was much like any other senior. I joined clubs, got involved with student council, joined the track team, and participated in senior activities. Because my son was a year old, he often joined me at after-school events and as you can imagine became well known within the senior class. I was ravishing through my prom pictures and smiling to myself. Even though I went alone, the images showed how much I'd enjoyed myself with my classmates. Boy was senior year fun.

While I was pregnant with Deon Jr., Big Deon was eighteen years of age, with a child on the way and not doing so well in school. Eventually, he stopped going to school and enrolled in a GED program. He also started working full time. He was a hard worker and was bringing in enough to supply the basic needs of Deon Jr. We had a good thing when I returned back to school after having the baby. His mom would watch the baby while he worked and I continued attending school. I eventually ended up getting a part-time job for myself that I worked after school hours. We were making it work, and it only seemed to make us closer, when we were together.

At some point, he ended up losing his job for fighting on the job, even though it was not a good thing I was understanding. Someone had attempted to challenge him on the job, and he handled it like a man. After losing his job, he disappeared for a while, and we would only talk over the phone. Between taking care of Deon Jr. and going to school, I never really made too much of a fuss about the way things were. I believed that he "had us" no matter what. Through conversation, he let me know he was staying with a relative in a nearby city. He would come and go, and I had no idea what he was doing, I was just happy to see him when he did come to town. Time passed, and this routine continued.

One night I woke up to my phone going off. It was a two-way so, you could hear multiple people on the line. Through the chirp, I could hear the laughter of girls. They were asking me who I was and in so many words letting me know that Deon was with them. They were actually two-waying me from a phone that I had given him. I didn't go on too much about it, because our son was asleep next to me in the bed. I waited until the next day to contact him. He told me that it was one of his girl cousins playing on his phone. I had no reason not to believe him, so I did, and we moved on.

This was not my first encounter with something like this. Early on in our relationship, there was a girl we attended school with, who reached out to me to let me know that they were, in fact, talking to each other. Because he and I were only talking, I never made a big deal about it. It was high school, and people were always talking or making up things to start drama. We never had a discussion about it, and I choose not to let it get in the way of what we were building.

Being a young mother, and going to school took so much energy from me, I just didn't have the power to give too much more. Over the years I trained my mind to move on. I learned that power grows where it goes. Over the years my priority was to provide energy to some things and file the other ones in a place that I wanted to forget. This played a significant role in my success, as I perfected the act of maintaining tunnel vision when it came to reaching my goals. On the flip side of that, it also served as a deficit in other areas of my life. I feed my success with everything I had, and intimate social interactions with friends and family went to the waist side.

## Chapter Three

*"When you are a mother, your hopes and dreams revolve around giving your child the world. This is a most challenging position to be in. It can cause you to go places you never thought you'd go, do things you never thought you'd do, and forget things you never thought you'd forget."*

-Rickesha Rose-

When Deon Jr. was about ten months old, I received a call that shook up our world. It was a call letting me know that his father was in jail. I was not sure how to react. I waited to hear from him. When I finally spoke with him, he told me that there was a mix up between him and his cousin. I did not know any logistics surrounding the charges. I just believed him. Why waste energy trying to make sense of it? He remained in jail for some time, and we'd talk consistently. We also wrote back and forth. I had no idea when he was coming home and what the future held for us.

Months passed, and I ended up meeting someone, even though I never took what we had seriously. He was good company during this time in my life. We hung out a lot and just enjoyed each other's presence. I was enjoying it in every way I could. Towards the end of the year, Deon finally got out. When he did, he came straight to my mom's house. There wasn't any talk about whether or not we were going to be together, we just were. Anything that I thought I had going on while he was gone didn't matter. He was home now, and I was ok with that. Deon was who I loved, and he was little Deon's father. If nothing else we were a family.

The other guy did not take the transition well. One day we were hanging out, and the next day he was non-existent to me. He seemed to not understand how I could just break things off like that. There was a period of time where he didn't want to accept it. He would tell me that we had something, but I wasn't trying to hear any of it. I was in love with Deon. Deon found out about him, and I was honest. I told Deon that he was just a friend, and not who I wanted. He was distraught and let me know that this was not ok. I felt horrible, and even though we moved on past it, Deon found subtle ways to remind me of what I did. For years in our relationship, I allowed the guilt to convict me. I allowed what happened to hold me hostage to so much more than I deserved.

During my pregnancy, Deon had begun working. Being on probation meant that his life consisted of work home Deon Jr. and me. Things were good with us. At least I thought it so. We decided when I turned eighteen that we'd get our own apartment. He often talked about his frustration of paying bills at home with his mom and how he'd rather pay for his own bills. By this time, I was working and attending college, and we were willing to make it work.

Just seven months after graduating from high school, I gave birth to my beautiful baby girl. A'miracle they called her, and a hidden miracle she was. I had not had any formal prenatal care. The day I went into labor, I was given an ultrasound. I was informed that her an umbilical cord was wrapped around her neck, and I was to be prepped for an emergency c-section.

At 1:30 pm on December 29, I heard her take her 1st breath, delayed, yet taken. I had done it. I had been informed about how much of a high risk I was because of my age and, lack of medical care. God still saw fit to bless me. He blessed both of us with two completely healthy babies. I don't for one minute deny the grace in my life, this was not the outcome of me making all the right choices. Grace and mercy had carried me.

We were eighteen and twenty years of age, and we had a formed a whole family. I don't deny for one second that they we both wanted nothing more than to be an intact family for the sake of the children. For the next year, we struggled quite a bit finically, which caused a lot of tension between us. Our relationship had its ups and downs, and on the down days, we seemed to suffer more with each new responsibility. The nights began to become war zones as Deon came home really late. I'd call him numerous times, and he wouldn't pick up. He came back when he was ready and let me know I was tripping. I didn't have the energy to fight with him. I began training myself to forget about it. I wanted to forget the expectations I had for us and what a relationship should be. Besides we had other things to take care of.

His excuses would do. He had to work late, or his was spending time with his people, so I understood. It became apparent that he didn't want to spend his money paying bills, he liked to hang out and drink with his friends, even though we couldn't afford it. We continued to stay together and make it work. Working and going to school, while taking care of the kids, I had less and less energy to give to situations that did not help our current circumstances. I wanted nothing more than to be a family and take care of home.

The year after my daughter was born, he asked for my hand in marriage. I said "yes," even though I was in no rush to be married. After listening to him talk with his father, it had kind of been presented that this was what we were supposed to do. I knew that this was a big step. I didn't think I was ready, but I knew I loved Deon and our family.

Shortly after, I can recall being at the college in between classes while studying. He did not have any classes, but he occasionally hung out on campus with family and friends that he knew. While studying a girl reached out to me, on social media to tell me that she had been sleeping with him and she had even been in our apartment. She talked about what a mess it was and how she just wanted to let me know. I was never the woman to go back and forward with other women. Undoubtedly, I wanted them to hurt the way that I did, but I had a way with words. If I were going to say anything, I would cut as deeply as I possibly could. There was no in between with me at that time and my life. I was either going to let you have it unapologetically, or I was going to walk away. I was livid and embarrassed about the way the information had come to me. I took all that energy that I was feeling, and I immediately went to the student union where he was playing pool and hanging out. I dropped the ring in his lap and stormed off, with every intention of leaving him there looking as foolish as I felt.

He manages to come up with a reasonable explanation and somehow made me feel like, it was mainly my fault that he even ended up in the situation. During the time the incident took place, I was away in Miami celebrating my older brother's birthday. Every year I'd go to Miami with a group of friends, and just enjoy the nightlife. He told me that the girl had come by our house with his cousin and asked to use the bathroom, which is how she knew what our apartment looked like. He swore he didn't want her. Somehow he admitted that they had a past and that she was just mad that he had turned her down now. Holding on to hope and needing to believe him, I let it go and stayed committed to him. I'd soon forget all about it. However, marriage was not back on the table just yet. It was going to take more than that, he had managed to make me feel guilty about going to Miami without him, but I couldn't trust him. I was okay with leaving marriage off the table.

# Chapter Four

## Rollercoaster & Red Flags

*"It is evident to me that we create defenses to protect ourselves from the pain of our reality."*

-Rickesha Rose-

The next couple of years only got worse. He was in and out of jail or prison every year. He was always booked on drug charges that were "never his." We would be okay while he was away. Letters were always sweet and full of commitment and remorse. When he'd come home, the honeymoon would be great, but it didn't last long. I would catch him cheating, and he would manage to convince me that I was crazy. He would always make me believe that the women were the problem. I had been drinking the Kool-Aid so long that it was like water to me. Drinking the Kool-Aid was a term we used when a guy fed you sweet nothings, and it's what you want to hear, so you take it in. Drinking the Kool-Aid means to deny intuition and many times known facts.

One of the worst fights we had was outside his aunt's house. It was another confrontation about cheating and a screaming match, turned physical. I remember being dragged across the road and getting up to fight back. One of his cousins jumped between us, not really to stop the fight, but more so to protect him from me. I can't even remember how I ended up in that space. At that point in my life, I had begun to experience blacking out. Blacking out allowed things like this to happen. When I say blacking out I mean, I remember a fight, but nothing more than that. Moments in time vanished entirely from my memory.

After that we took a break, I was done! I did not want to be with him. I was in school and working and felt confident about taking care of myself. Eventually, he went to back to jail. It was becoming a continuing cycle. He would be out for a year and back in for a year. I wasn't used to the consistency of his absence. Of course, while he was away, he wrote me often, all sweet letters about how sorry he was about everything, and how he wanted to be a family. He told me that I was going to be his "Mrs.." Deep in my heart, I valued building a family with him over everything else. I eventually blocked out the incident and begin to make the trip to go see him in prison. I was really ready to be a single mother, that feeds the stereotype of a teen mother. I'd rather make it work with him than to be labeled.

It was time to forget. I ventured to forget what mattered most. I would forget respect, self-worth, and even my value as a woman.

Time passed, and we were back together. Whenever we'd fight, I'd try to break it off. He'd petition in his most sincere voice and tell me that's not what he wanted. I remember one time he said to me that he couldn't live without me and that he had actually considered suicide. I thought this was real love, and it scared me. Did I really have that type of influence over his life? I believed that this was a true testament to how badly he loved me.

Over the next couple of years, we continued to live together and struggle together. We were committed to each other and committed to being a family. I was working so hard to not fall into the statistic of a teen mother, and I was determined to finish school. I was determined to have that picture perfect family. My energy directed towards being successful and outrunning the perception.

I told myself that even if he didn't make me happy, staying with him would be worth the sacrifice if the kids were delighted. I had vowed to forget so much that happened. My defense mechanism worked overtime to keep my focus. The rebellious spirit that existed in me worked to my advantage when it came to my studies. If I could just finish this class, get that job, complete this degree, I would show them I wasn't dumb, and that there was more to me than just being a teen mother.

After that, the fighting subsided a bit. I was committed to finishing school and being a mother. There was a point in our relationship where I checked out. I was set on proving others wrong about me and the life that had been outlined for me. With my head in my books and working two, sometimes three jobs, Deon's actions began to fade in the background. It didn't matter, I was doing what I needed for myself.

A year before I was due to graduate from college, Deon got into an unfortunate accident on his way home from work. I received a call while I was at work telling me that "someone was on the ground." That was the worst thing they could have ever done. Those words sent my whole body into shock. I left work in a panic and rushed to be with him. Everything that goes through your mind at the thought of someone you love dying went through my mind. I was a mess. All I wanted was for everything to be right with us.

## Chapter Five

### Recovery & Ring

*"The purpose of recovery is to heal what has been broken."*

-Rickesha Rose-

When Deion was in that accident, so many things ran through my mind. I was an emotional wreck at just the thought of things ending like that. I was ready for a change, a change between Deon and me. We had our problems but we had our good days, and he was all I knew. I was ready to work on us at all costs.

Seeing him in the hospital, changed my perspective on how I looked at us and the things that we had been through. Sitting in that ER room, I began to think long and hard about the future of our relationship. I couldn't see myself without him. I couldn't see myself with anyone else. We had been through so much. The sight of him in this condition was overwhelming. I was hurting. Looking back on this moment I'm not sure if I was emotional because of his health, or because I wanted everything to be right with us. I did not want to regret anything. I never wanted to be that girl "wishing" wishing that I had done this or said that. It was time to forget the past. I was ready to reconnect the way we were when we first started dating. During his time of recovery, we had a serious talk about us, he had not changed his mind about marrying me. I wanted to be married to him.

As the recovery process began, so did the planning. We talked more and more about making things official. He went through a few months of physical therapy, but he made it out with no long-term, life-threatening damage.

It was our time. We had survived the kid stuff. It was time to move on and be adults. We were going to have our happy ever after. He received a nice settlement from the accident, and he spent the money spoiling me. We took trips and planned our wedding. 2012 was a year of total bliss for me. I completed my degree, which was a degree that I initially didn't set out to attain. My goal when I started was to at least get my Associate's degree and see what would happen from there. I had been told going off to a university was not a realistic goal for me. When I finished my degree at the community college, it also became a state college that now offered Bachelor's degrees. Receiving my Bachelor's degree was one of the most significant accomplishments of my life. There were many semesters that I cried and wanted to give up. My drive to finish what I started was stronger than anything any professor could have thrown at me. Receiving my Bachelor's degree also led to a job offer within the organization I was working for at the time. It was a smooth transition and made my resume look ten times better.

All things considered, Deon and I made our final commitment to a small wedding, with close friends and family. I said "I do" in a botanical garden & with my high school sweetheart. I was on cloud nine with no intentions to come down. Forget everything that had to happen before this. I had done precisely what I set out to do. I was not another statistic. Not only did I graduate from college, but I had also married the father of my children. I wanted nothing more than to break the barriers. I wanted nothing about my children's life to say, that their parents were teen parents. This was a significant accomplishment and at the time, worth the things I'd had learned to forget.

Life was good. I had no complaints. I had to work hard to get the picture perfect family and picture-perfect lifestyle, before the age of twenty-five. No one could have ever told me that I would have to come down and prepare myself for a hard landing.

It sometimes seems as if life goes on an emotional rollercoaster. I continued to tell myself, that we must take the good with the bad. The good teaches us to forget the bad and hold on to the hope that it will be good again. I mean what's life without hope?

# Chapter Six

## Happily ever...maybe

*"You hear it time and time again, but until you are in this moment, you can't really comprehend the meaning " the honeymoon was over."*

-Rickesha Rose-

They say nothing is perfect, but some moments in my life felt pretty close to it. My little family was the closest thing to perfect in my eyes. Deon Jr. was now six, and A'miracle was four. We were attending church and working, such that we finally had a little finical breathing room. We began taking more family trips. Even so, the things in his past always lingered close. It was hard to believe that Deon's ways had changed. I felt that he was still connected to his past actions. The guys that he would frequently hang around never seemed genuine enough to care about our family. I never got close enough to really know any of them either. He was always telling them that I wasn't friendly, but these guys seem so shady. It was hard for me to believe that anything he was doing with them was in the best interest of our family. On the surface, it appeared as if I just didn't want him hanging out. The reality was that I had a lot to feel insecure about, and I didn't want him hanging out the way he did.

Things didn't add up, and my intuition made me completely parionard. We were attending church regularly and consistently told that the first year of the marriage would be rough.

When he lost his job, it became evident that he was having a hard time. He would make comments to let me know I could do better than being with him. I would do all that I could to build him up and help him get back on his feet. I wouldn't talk about my job or anything I was accomplishing in my career. I was doing everything I could to keep him happy. Inside I was slowly losing it, trying to find my way in a cloud of smoke. With voices in my ear telling me this is just how it is, I began painting the picture that if I stayed strong and stayed the course, the smoke would clear. Everything in me wanted to believe that was true. Life can make you bitter, you no longer taste the sweetness in the air. The battle of the mind is a real thing.

I was enjoying my new position and adjusting well to a very high demanding job. I was by far the youngest one in my department, and would always get reminded that I was such a baby whenever age was brought up. It didn't bother me very much as I felt it be an achievement to be just as qualified to perform the job alongside my colleagues. I had one particular co-worker who took me a little more than the others. He was always accommodating when I had questions and would often volunteer to mentor and me, which included shadowing him in the field. I really appreciated him and assumed he was just a nice guy. I believed that he was the same way with everyone, until the day he came on to me. He reached out to me one day after work to express that he had become fond of me. I ended the call with an "ok?" Completely shocked I pretend the call never happened. I was blown away, I felt this man was out of my league. He was older, very handsome, and well liked by everyone. He had the type of energy that makes you take notice of him when he enters a room. Not to mention the fact that he was married, and so was I. Even with everything I had been through with my husband, I had never stepped out on him and didn't see the point in doing so. It felt like it was more trouble than it was worth. I was too busy trying to keep him happy and take care of our family the best way I knew how.

My immediate response was to tell my husband. I wanted to tell him without angering him, as tension in our home had yet to subside. He was not working at the time, yet spent a lot of time away from home. I began by trying to set up some alone time together. Time passed, and the conversation was never had. It felt horrible. It was like we were living together but in separate worlds. To be married and feel so alone has to be one of the worst feelings.

Neglect must have been all over my demeanor as I continued to push through the days, juggling the new position, the kids, and my husband's mood swings. My co-worker and I begin to frequently eat lunch together. I told myself that our time spent was completely innocent as I had made my intentions clear.

One day I was coming home from work and received a call that my husband had been arrested. His brother reported that not only was he going to jail but that a woman had called the police on him for hitting her. I guess my number got passed on that night, as I received a call from the woman who wanted to "talk." She felt that she needed to tell me that her and my husband were planning to say to me that she was pregnant. Apparently, that didn't end well, and the altercation between them began. At that moment I didn't feel guilty about entertaining the guy at work. I was so torn. I wish I had done more.

## Chapter Seven

*"Is numb truly a feeling when you truly feel nothing?"*
-Rickesha Rose-

My body was in motion, but there were no feelings of association with anything I was doing. When I talked to my husband, he told me the girl who had made the accusations was lying, and that she was mad that he didn't want her. By now I knew the script, but I didn't care anymore. What was the point in fighting, arguing or anything at this point? I rationalized it all by telling myself that if he were going to cheat, then so would I. I was tired of being embarrassed and feeling like I was doing something wrong. So the next time someone tried to tell me he was cheating, I would be prepared to say "I'm doing me." That would keep me from looking like a fool. I became numb and began to do things I didn't agree with. I began to vent to other guys from my past, and occasionally I'd have guys reach out to me, who knew exactly what was going on the entire time. Those so-called "friends" who I always questioned, couldn't wait to share the dirt with me. Imagine that!

How did I end up here? I didn't care about anything or anyone. I loved my children and never stepped out of my role of being a mother, but the savage in me was awake. I only aim to get what I wanted and if others got hurt in the process, so be it. I didn't care about being judged. In fact, I wanted people to know I wasn't taking no sh*t. Forget their feelings, no one had looked out for me.

It's crazy how things play out in a relationship when infidelity is involved. You replay every scenario in your head, piece together unaccounted for time, and start to question the loyalty of everyone around you. I had to shake this, I was headed down a road of destruction. I hated feeling hopeless, and I was ready to move on. However, I knew my ability to trust would never be the same again. After two months of completely ignoring the fact that my husband was in jail, not accepting any calls and refusing to go see him, I began to miss him. I felt I had done enough dirt and needed to see him. When I went to see him, I ran into his cousin in the lobby. She told me that she had called for me to come in to see her cousin. I told her that it wasn't me, but she insisted that she had called for me. Eager to prove that she was right she went on and on to eventually call a name. The name was one that I recognized, but it wasn't mine. It was the same girl who he claimed was crazy. Imagine that. This happening before the visit even began. When he came out, I couldn't wait to share the news I had just learned. He was same on Deon. He had a story for me, and it somehow held me responsible yet again. He told me he only called her because I wouldn't take his calls. The cousin had already confirmed that the girl had indeed supplied him with what he needed to get by in jail. I understood and was more upset with myself about the things I had done. We both spent the majority of that visit breaking down and apologizing for how we were hurting each other. This time unlike before I wanted to know the ins and outs of why he was there. Apparently, he had a pending warrant that was over a year old. He had five pending charges.

After our heart to heart in the visitation room, I went back to just being his wife and began to make arrangements to bond him out so he would come home and we could work on us. We were still in our first year of marriage. I believed that the elder women in the church were telling me, that all this was an attack on our marriage and that we were going to get through this. I finally told him about the guy at work, reassuring him that I was done and that it would all stop.

When I reached out to my co-worker, he got upset and reminded me that this wasn't just about me. We were escaping both of our realities together. I had confided in him and told him so much while my husband was away. He had enough information to make me feel like I was making a mistake. I felt like maybe I was selfish to just end what we had.

Things did not get better at home, after my confession. Deon could not take the thought of me being with another man. It was the ultimate betrayal to him. I had stood firm and forgiven his infidelity repeatedly, but he was convinced that this was different and he didn't know if he could get over it.

While Deon was away, my co-worker had completed some work for an event and had been asked to supply services for one of Deon's relatives, even though I forbid it. It didn't stop him. It was work for him, so he took it like it was any other job. One typical Sunday we gathered at his aunt's house as we had done many Sundays before. Everyone was eating, and the kids were playing, like we always did after church services. His cousin brought up my co-worker and referenced the work he had done for her party. Before I knew it Deon's family was seeing another part of him that reflected his insecurities. I remember getting in the car and trying to leave and him slapping the window with such force. I remember his mom trying to get him to just back away. The steam coming from him was so prevalent. By now everyone was observing what was going on. An uncle finally got him to walk away, and I left, thoroughly embarrassed and partially feeling guilty.

    He didn't come home that night. Eventually, he came back, and we moved on like nothing happened. The kids were happy to see him, as they remembered coming to their aunt's house with him, but leaving without him. They were delighted, and so was I. It didn't matter how many times he had stayed out late, a part of me always felt better when he returned. There were so many nights I dreaded getting a call that he was in jail or something worse. My anger would eventually subside to be just being happy he made it back home. For the next couple of days, we spent a lot of time together at home. He was showing me that he wanted to make things right with us.

## Chapter Eight

### I Had to run

*"They say doing the same thing over and over and expecting a different result is the definition of insanity."*
-Rickesha Rose-

I refer to my "learning days" as the days where it took me longer to grasp reality. I thank God for a sister, that not only supports me in any way she can but one who has never belittled me. She has held me up, even when I didn't know I was falling. The covering has not gone unnoticed.

After spending the day out and about, we decided to make the night a movie night in. We had gotten everything we needed and were home getting settled. We had even gotten a bottle of wine. When we got back, we realized that we didn't have a wine cork. With a suspended license and out on bond, Deon convinced me to allow him to run to the store to get one. We had been working on me not being so controlling and trusting him. "Less than ten minutes, I'll be right back," he said. Those were his last words before taking off.

After the first hour, I began to worry and panic, as I had done so many nights before. My mind raced, and I was praying everything was alright. It just so happened that I left my charger in the car for my phone. I did not think that I would need it before he returned. Luckily I had a work phone that I could use if I really needed to. Something told me to go outside, and as I began walking toward the main road, I could see police lights. They had pulled a car over. The vehicle was at least a half a mile away from me. As I got closer, I could see that there was a tow truck there also. I finally let it soak in what I was seeing. I got on the phone and called 911. Panicking I told the operator that I thought my car was being towed, but I wasn't sure why or what was going on. It was confirmed that it was, in fact, my car. I begin to plead with the operator, and I was informed that the driver was going to jail for having drugs in the car. I was told that the arresting officer had tried to make contact with me but was unsuccessful and had made the call to have the vehicle impounded. If you have ever seen an episode of Miami Tow, this moment in my life qualified for its own priemer. This turned into the ugliest process I had ever been through. After talking to the officer and tracking down where my car was located, only to be told that the shop was closed and I could not get my car until Monday. This meant that I had to pay them for each night they held it due to the office being closed. I ended up waiting for three days and spending money I didn't have to get back something I should've never lost.

    Meanwhile, the Kool-Aid he had been giving me stayed the same. On the other end of yet another collect call was the same old' Deon, with a calm and collective "hey bae" pleading his case. According to him, he hadn't done anything wrong. He "was giving his homeboy a ride home" and the drugs didn't belong to him. Apparently honoring street code was more valuable than the position he had put his wife and children in yet again. In short, he had made the executive decision to take the wrap for the drugs since he was the driver.

This time I couldn't bond him out even if I wanted to. I did get him a lawyer. We discussed the possibility of him getting seven years and how that would affect the kids if he had taken a chance with a trial. The lawyer got two of the charges dropped and he eventually only served ten months in prison.

This was beginning to take a toll on me emotionally, financially as well as professionally. I found myself lying to my colleagues, socializing less and less with others, and especially my co-workers. Whenever we talked about our spouses or our home lives, I'd lie and say my husband was away on business. It sounded a lot better than saying he was in prison. The problem was that like any other lie, you have to be creative to keep the lie going. I was hating who I was becoming, trying to hold together a fairy tale that did not exist.

## Chapter Nine

*"You learn to run from what you feel if you're constantly in motion. Adrenaline takes over, and your emotions dissipate."*

-Rickesha Rose-

My best friend has a way with advice when we're having a heart to heart. Whenever I'm trying to figure out what to do, she is always sure not to tell me what to do, but to guide me towards a decision. I'd go on and on just for her to say "aye man live your life." It was never too much and always came with a reassurance that she was there for me, no matter what I decided. I needed that reassurance for what was to come.

This time when Deon came home, I was sure that all the bad was behind us. We were coming up towards our second anniversary. I believed if nothing else we had passed the test. I booked a cruise to celebrate and to say "let's start over and put the past behind us." We started attending church on a regular basis as a family again. I began to feel the way I did when we first got married. He was so sweet and kind with his ways and most importantly with his words. We had a disagreement that left both of us heated. Shortly after, he came to me and apologized, showing me that he had been reading his Bible and that he didn't want to fight. This honeymoon lasted all of two to three weeks.

Before I knew it, he was drinking and smoking again. After saying he was done, the late nights in the streets began again. After about a month or so of being home, I discovered a text message from a girl saying she wanted to see him. While upset and confused I confronted him right away. He must have had this story prepared as he quickly responded, stating that the girl didn't even know him. He went on to say that he had let his cousin use his phone earlier and that she was probably reaching back out to him.

I let it go. I was tired of having the same fight about the same things, just to end up in the same place. I was tired of fighting. The hope in me wanted to believe him. As time went on the truth was sure to reveal itself. He was cheating again. I knew I needed to make a change on my end if I want to a real difference in my life. I realize I was holding on to hope.

# Chapter Ten

### Go Your Way

My brother in law became a secret guardian in my life, I'm confident that I talk to him as much as I talk to my sister. He would give me advice about men. It is so helpful to get advice from a man that has no intentions other than seeing you at your best. This undeniably became one of the best scenarios that a woman could have.

The pace of my life was becoming too much to hide from my family, friends and more importantly myself. I was functioning within a dysfunctional life. After this, we mutually agree that we should live apart. The reality was we had been living in a dysfunctional manner and out of order long enough. The order of the household had never been the way we both felt it should be. I believed that the man was supposed to lead in every aspect. He was supposed to guide us financially, emotionally and spiritually. We may have not done everything in order, but we did have a firm belief in the biblical version of marriage. He claimed he had never made a way for himself.

He decided to go live with his brother for a while, to eventually get on his feet and rebuild the structure of our family to become the head of our home. Overall I managed and provided a sufficient level of stability for the sake of my children. We were living in a three bedroom, two bath home with a garage and plenty of yard space for the children.

I moved out of the house into a two bedroom apartment, paying the same for rent. I cared more about the peace, I was desperately seeking. While living apart, he'd make sure to let me know that he was watching me. I wasn't sure why he went out of his way to do so. I had nothing to hide. He confirmed my suspicions by calling me one night while I was out, to let me know he didn't see my car. He wanted to know what I was doing. It didn't take long for me to discover that he was staying with a female. Naturally, he denied it and managed to resort to "if it was so" it was because I had put him out, so he had no other options. He acknowledged that he had agreed to the separation because he knew that's what I wanted anyway.

I was done drinking the Kool-Aid at this point. No matter how the situation began or ended, it was my fault. I didn't care anymore. This merry go round was getting old to me, I was outgrowing it. The song by Fantasia "Even Angels" was getting me by. I could learn to fly on my own. This couldn't be God's plan for my life.

You never know how strong you can be until you are in a situation where being strong is the only choice you have.

## Chapter Eleven

### Final Straw

*"When you're fighting a battle that is not yours, you're in a no-win situation."*

-Rickesha Rose-

**Seek God and hold onto to your peace.**

I was so confused. The smoke had yet to clear, and I needed to breathe fresh air. I began going to a different church. I was crying out to God to fix my marriage. I felt like I had failed. The number of women was steadily increasing, and part of me felt like I had pushed him away. Every morning I would start my day crying, reaching out in prayer just to get out the bed. I was trying to keep him and the kids happy. I was sacrificing to save our family picture perfect. Attending gatherings and events as a family through the day and him returning back to the things he did at night was just too much. The girls would make it so apparent that they were sleeping together. One day I had enough, and I confronted a girl openly on social media. I didn't spare any choice words. Her response was to post pictures of the two of them together. It was the release I needed. I wanted his family to see what he had been up to. I couldn't take it anymore. I was free from what was eating away at me up behind closed doors.

He had been seeing her for quite some time. Seeing the photos only confirmed what I already knew. My first response was to feel relief. I guess I needed the confirmation that I wasn't crazy. Some words were exchanged, and truth be told the entire thing was embarrassing. I never wanted to be that girl. I never wanted to be seen fighting and giving the world something to talk about.

To my surprise, his family, as well as mine, was more supportive and understanding of my position then I could have ever imagined. They reached out with sincere prayers, apologizes and a different level of knowledge from one woman to another. Regardless of what the connection was between us, they showed regard for me. The hard part was preparing my children for what was happening.

I learned that life is unpredictable, and you never know what is coming next, don't ever get too comfortable. Always be ready for a change.

## Separation

After that, I decided that we were officially separated. I began to pray to God that his will be done, and not my own. I started to demand that God fix it or move it. FIX IT OR MOVE IT! I cried to God. I wanted so badly to make the women go away. I still believed then that we would have a story about how much we'd overcome. FIX IT OR MOVE IT! I continued to pray. As time went on things on got worse. My prayer was being answered, just not in the way I wanted.

At the time I didn't get it. With every prayer came more exposure. I didn't have to look for evidence, things were literally hitting me right in the face.

One day after coming back from a family trip, he was unloading the car, or so I thought. My phone rang, and it was another one. She was yelling that I needed to get him and tell him to stay away from her. When he returned, I asked a simple "why"? After an amazing family vacation, this is how it had to end? He blew up on me and told me that I was stupid and would believe anything. I asked for my keys and asked him to leave. He refused and continued to plead his case, "another crazy girl" he proclaimed. I was deaf to everything he was saying, "Give me my damn keys," I exclaimed. I was tired. I had no more fight in me, not for this. Knowing the kids were right in the next room, I wanted nothing more than to not fight with him. After having an arguing match and me threatening to call the police, he finally gathered his things and headed to the door. He was kicking furniture and slapping the window next to the door forcefully, to cause a startle reaction in not only in me but also the kids who were now in the doorway of their room. The looks on their faces let me know that this was never what I wanted for them. I didn't realize it at the time, but I was about to begin a journey that would change our lives drastically. I was willing to do whatever it took to make sure they saw better, even if I had to do it on my own.

## Chapter Twelve

### (He thought I was worth keeping)

*"There is freedom in complete surrender."*
-Rickesha Rose-

It was Tuesday evening prayer, I didn't even make it to the altar. My knees hit the ground, right in the pew on the back row. I began to cry a cry like never before. Lord I NEED YOU NOW! I don't know what else to do. I couldn't tell you who came and left or how long I was there, the Prophet spoke into my life and said, told me that God was not going to move my situation at that moment. He explained that it was time for me to come out of it. I was sick mentally, emotionally and physically and I blamed myself. How did I end up here? I loved this man, even on his worst days. From long rides to prisons in the middle of nowhere, sleeping in my car, and dragging my kids inside prisons to dealing with their broken hearts when visitation time came to an end. I had held in my tears, stood firm through job loss, accidents, multiple release dates, living one letter at a time, to end up here. I was not perfect, but I didn't deserve this.

God had been covering me the entire time. I didn't know, and I didn't feel it. Each time he went away I was covered. Each sign and cycle that I ignored, he covered me.

My repeated prayer to God, to let his will be done and not my own was manifesting. "Let your will be done, and not my own," became my daily mantra. That next month I received a job offer for a job in another city. To make this move, I had to trust God completely.

When I was younger, I watched movies about women and men, who left town with what could fit in their car, not knowing what was to come. They would be flying on faith and prayer, only knowing that it was time for a change. I had no idea this happened in real life, and furthermore that it would happen in my life.

I left everything. I placed my belongings in storage and made arrangements for my kids to stay with my sister until I could secure a place. God had put me in a position where I needed to trust him completely. Throughout many confirmations and revelations, God had shown me that I thought I was in control of my life and the choices I had made for myself. This was not the plan he had for me. Leaving my kids with my sister was one of the hardest decisions I ever made, but I knew they were in good hands. I also knew that what was about to happen next, was necessary. I could only give them my best at my best.

And so my journey began securing a job in St. Petersburg, Florida. I had a cousin I was living with in Tampa, but for the most part, I was alone away from everything I had known. I was entirely plucked from my comfort zone, but it didn't feel wrong. God was reassuring me that he had me. He gave me peace and continued to show me how Deon, now my ex, had so much control over me. I found myself taking back control of things I never knew I had lost. God began to give me a bird's eye view that I didn't have before. I started to pick up on his patterns. We would go for long periods of time without talking, and he would conveniently show up when things were going well. He'd allow me to pray for him, and let me know he didn't want to be where he was, yet his actions never match his words. I learned to hear him but not react. His interaction with the kids became scarce. The less I responded, the more bothered he became. His visits became farther and farther apart.

Now I can say the reason I thought was a good reason to make it work, was the very reason I left. I wanted my kids to grow up in a loving family, yet they were getting the complete opposite. It didn't matter whether it was happening behind closed doors or in their faces, it was not what I wanted for them. I knew the moment I settled for it, I would be giving them the ok to do the same, and that I couldn't live with that.

It wasn't easy to let go, and see that together was more harm than good. Today I thank God for freeing me from the things that held me bonded.

I got a tattoo with 2 Corinthians 3:17 imprinted on my shoulders to remind me, that where the spirit of the Lord is, there is freedom!

NOW, WHAT?

Now I wish I could say that I rode off into the sunset, never looked back and lived happily ever after. If I did, I'd be giving you a distorted view of reality. The reality is that I looked back several times. I can, however, tell you that I never went back. I had begun a journey to get my pearls back.

In life, women and young girls are given or accrue pearls to wear usually for special occasions.

As women, our pearls are the beautiful lessons that we learn in our lives. My pearls are my integrity, and how I presented myself as a mother. As time moved forward, I learned to add lessons to my string of pearls. I placed a value on my purpose, my joy, and my peace. These were my pearls, and I became determined not to leave the house without them.

As I began to heal, I started to discover, that I had a purpose. I also learned that my purpose was more significant than the trials I've experienced. I realized that I had a story to share and a new perception of life.

As a life coach, I love empowering women to not only discover their pearls in life but tap into obtaining them, tapping into the things they value the most. This is not the same for every woman. I want to share with you the things I discovered, to live a life of freedom, peace, and purpose. The healing process was not easy, and some days I still wonder how I ended up in some of those places. I learned that if you are not aware, your past will hold you hostage. The shame and the hurt will make you believe that you can't recover. The battle of the mind is real. You must understand that what you dwell on and give energy to manifests in your life. If you focus on the past, you will live your life in the past, but if you discover your worth, and your value and focus on honoring and loving yourself, your energy will follow.

## *Conclusion*

It is incredible the weight that is lifted when we not only tell our story but indeed accept the story. We cannot go back in time and change the chapters or rip out individual pages. We can, however, look at the story in a different light, acknowledge the hiccups, and headaches, without diminishing the beauty mixed. You never know it was a bad time if you didn't know what a good time felt like. Acknowledging and being grateful for having a story to tell is a blessing in its own, ugly as it may seem. There is beauty among the ashes. Telling my account was not a platform to point fingers and play the blame game. I was not looking for a pity party, and I can only pray that I haven't ruffled a few feathers. Sharing my story, was not for me, I already knew what happened. Someone needed to know that it happened, and "I Still." I made some poor choices but "I Still." I fell a few times but "I Still." Not only did "I Still" but "He Still" God still loves me. One of my favorite gospel songs is Travis Greene's, "He waited." He waited just for me! There is nothing in my past that disqualifies me from living in my best life and walking in my purpose.

As I began my journey, after my discovery. God started to give me a revelation about things I needed to deal with within myself before I genuinely stepped into what he had for me. I share with you the lessons I learned and the process that helped me breathe again, and see life without the smoke. As I begin to take these steps, I started to ask myself how I wanted to show up in the world. Each day was a new day to get ready for whatever was next. As women, we tend to put a lot of energy into how we get ready, whether that be just for the night, or for a journey. The concept of bringing my pearls became so imperative for me. I needed to show up at my best. I need to bring my value and my worth wherever I go. As mentioned, pearls represent royalty, grace, and cost. I share with you now the steps I took that changed my life and pushed me to an unexplainable level of peace and self-worth.

**Embrace Your Truth**

For all of us that is something different. Every blue moon I call my sister and start the conversation with "I have something to tell you". Usually she responds by saying "Oh God". I have proclaimed boldly that I had been on this journey of facing all truths in my life. Some made me laugh, some made me cry, some changed my life. This was true not only for me but for everyone connected to me. Some have been revealed, and others are going to take some time. But I did it. There is a different level of freedom you feel, when you don't live a life full of secrets, and you let light shine in those dark places.

**What are some truths you've yet to face?**

_____
_____
_____
_____
_____
_____
_____
_____
_____
_____
_____
_____
_____

**Don't just go through the process, grow through the process.**

Life is constantly in transition. Some move faster than others. Some feel better than others. Once you realize you're either going into something, in the middle of something or coming out of something, you determine that it is all a part of living. How you handle it makes the difference. Learn to find the beauty on the ugly days, you might as well get something out of it.

**Where are you on your journey? Can you find the beauty in it?**

_____
_____
_____
_____
_____
_____
_____
_____
_____
_____
_____
_____

**Life can be hard, sometimes it hurts.**

One of the best things I could have ever done, was admit when I was hurting, I used to be so content on not feeling. There came a time in my life where I decided I'd rather be completely broken, than continually breaking. A broken vessel is easier to reconstruct. When your the one that is pretending to not be broken, holding all the pieces together, you become more vulnerable to the simplest touch. Life can be hard, and we are human. Things will hurt, but you can't heal if you don't admit to even being hurt in the first place.

Here I want you to admit to yourself that sometimes "life is hard". Are there areas in your life that still hurt? If so what are they? Who can help you through this?

_____
_____
_____
_____
_____
_____
_____
_____
_____
_____
_____
_____
_____

**Understand your boundaries.**

As a married woman I had boundaries. As a single woman I have boundaries. I have learned to understand my triggers. I know there are certain people I can't talk to, and that there are certain things I'm not going to do, so I don't end up in situations I don't want to be in. Understand that my heart was vulnerable after my separation. I was wise enough to realize I had to set boundaries with how I interacted with others.

*What areas in your life do you need to set boundaries?*

**Just because you can, doesn't mean you should.**

A wise man taught me that emotions are real but they are not reliable. One of the worst things you can do is react off your emotions, knowing there is a chance you'll regret it later. Your emotions will make you give away pieces of yourself that are still healing, resulting in a setback in your healing process. Temptation is real, but so is regret. Beyoncé told us, "always stay gracious, the best revenge is your paper". If I could remix that I'd replace paper, with pearls, remember your values.

Do you allow your emotions to rule you? *If so how can you change that?*

**Identify your pearls.**

Take the time to identify what matters to you. What are those things that you sacrifice for the sake of keeping others happy? Is it your joy or your peace? Are you dimming your light, or scared to walk in purpose? Understand that there is nothing in life that you can do that makes you unworthy of your royalties, your happiness, or your freedom. Jesus Christ died for all our sins. All is forgiven. Discover what your pearls are, and when you do, don't leave without them. Don't forget your pearls.

*What are your pearls?*

RICKESHA ROSE

## ABOUT THE AUTHOR

Rickesha, known for beating the odds and for boldness, focuses on her faith and not fitting into societal norms. Shocking the world by managing to graduate from college, after becoming a two- time teen mom, she knows what it feels like to be judged, and counted out.

As a certified Life Coach, Rickesha uses her experiences, skills, and education to empower and educate others to a place of freedom and endless possibilities. Aside from writing, speaking, teaching and being an advocate for teens and women, her organization Becoming Concrete is designed to help individuals build a solid foundation no matter where they are in life, or what has happened in their past.

Rickesha founded Becoming Concrete Enrichment Services. With an offering of online courses, workshops, one on one coaching and youth enrichment services, Becoming Concrete empowers individuals to stand on a solid foundation with everything they are made of and to discover that they have a purpose in their story.

Recognized as a phenomenal resource for teens and women, Rickesha speaks at local churches, group homes, advocacy groups, and is dedicated to sharing and empowering.

## **CONNECT WITH RICKESHA ROSE**
IG : rickesha_rose
Author Page: rickesharose.com
Blog PG : https://bcomingconcrete.wordpress.com

www.ingramcontent.com/pod-product-compliance
Lightning Source LLC
Chambersburg PA
CBHW052112070526
44584CB00017B/2451